Thoughts & Words:

A Poem Collection

Reneil D. Campbell

First published in 2021 by:

Reneil Damion Campbell

ISBN: 9798728090946

Cover photo by: Tuson Photography

Artwork by: Josh-Neal Taylor

"Reneil, keep writing. Live, love, experience life fully, and translate it into beautiful sentences. Continue filling the universe with amazing content" **Shaneele A. Ebanks.**

Introduction

Writing is a beautiful and wonderful experience; it has become my voice, peace, and solitude. I have been writing pieces of poetry from the tender age of 10 years old. However, I have never shared any with the world.

Most of the following pieces were written more than ten years ago and will take you on a short journey from heartbreak to everlasting love.

As you read my thoughts and words, I hope you will find joy, peace, solace, and escape.

Reneil D. Campbell

Thoughts & Words

Content

-Heartbreak

-Escape

-The Truth

-Afraid

-Let go

-Faith

-Exceptional

-The Proposal

-Everlasting Love

Others

Heartbreak

It hurts like hellfire, even though we know not for sure what
that is like,
but deep down, we think we have experienced it because we
feel it deep down in our souls; the surface of the sun does not
burn this much, I know it, you know it, the universe knows it,
every organ, every bone, every nerve, every cell hurts, there is
no more incredible pain than a real heartbreak.

You want to scream; you want to fall and die,
Jesus! Why. Why did this happen? Why did this happen to
me?
This pure soul, so divine, so faithful, so loyal, so... so good,
wicked and cruel world, this world of love,
I want no part of it, get away from me!
You selfish and heart-wrenching demon, go back to the depths
of Tartarus.

You will not win; one day, you will be brought to justice; you
evil and loathing speck of unnecessary ordeal called love; why
do you bring so much joy and peace?
But then you completely transform into the darkest of days,
the blackest of nights; so dangerous, so so uggghh.

I will defeat you, conquer you,
soon I will bloom flowers of light, I will become a beautiful
butterfly,
Fly, fly, fly away,
far away from this heartbreak.

Escape

Now I know the words to every sad song, each note that plays,
I feel it to my core,
the wind, oh the wind, I never knew it felt this good,
so divine, so fresh, yes! I am learning, learning to cope.

Hope, faith, friends... family,
I keep them close, closer than the skin on my bones, yes, yes, I
am getting there slowly, but ha ha, oh so indeed.

You thought you destroyed me, oh no! I am still here,
fighting, writing, singing, recovering,
I will survive, I am surviving without you,
I am making it without you.

I continue to sing like a bird, soar, above it all, my secret place
no longer your embrace,
but with my pen, I now write of joy, peace... Escape.

The Truth

What did you say? That you are on a journey to find love,
my best wishes as you go on your way,
but may I dare say that love is like your eyes; at times, we
may forget that they are right in front of us.

I am crazy, you say, you've been searching all of your days,
I'm afraid I have to disagree, yes that is what I say,
you have been looking too far away, in places you know not
of,
when love itself is staring at you, yes in your very face.

I am dreaming, you say, living a fairytale,
my friend. I don't mean to be a busy body or rude,
but let me remove the veil from your face; I charge you, open
your eyes, and come back to reality because love smiles
gracefully at everyone.

Mad man, I am true because I believe I speak the truth; you
don't want to hear any more?
My friend, hear me out; you don't have to search for love; it is
within you.

Afraid

I am afraid, I am in awe; how can one be so assertive?
Since I've met you, I feel at ease; everything will be all
right.

Is this feeling for real? Will it fade away?
Will we become strangers as time goes by?
Or will it turn into something magical?

My heart wants to believe every word, but I have heard it
all before; what makes you different?
I am afraid.

My heart is scared of giving it's all again,
to have it torn apart,
please, please, please, please,
Do not break my heart… I am afraid.

Let go

I know what you are going through; even though I may laugh
at times,
that is my way of showing that I care; it is my way of keeping
you near.

I know what it is like,
but you have to put up a fight
with all your might,
and I'll be there to help you, to make things bright.

Sometimes the past seems overwhelming,
but with time and someone to talk to, it will not seem
unending; it makes sense too to put things behind and forget;
the past can ruin you if you let it.

I know it is not easy, but at least try,
and if you fail, try again and again until you get it right; it is
just life; deal with it
and let go, and I promise it will be okay.

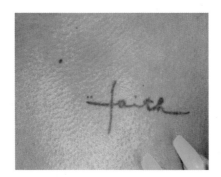

Faith

I no longer look to the past; I look to you, my future. Will you
be there until the end? You will be here always... Faith

, I never knew happiness until I met you; your smile makes
everything worthwhile; your presence takes me to heaven
I will be happy with you forever... Faith

: There is no mountain too high; there is no battle that I cannot
fight,
no monster too big to conquer; you will give me strength,
power, power... Faith

We will make it together, no storm, no weather
can keep you away from me, we will find each other no matter
what... Faith

: We will love each other forever, be together,

make it, and... Faith

Exceptional

I like the way you reason,

I believe it doesn't come about by season,

I like your outlook on life
especially your belief in the earth becoming a paradise.

I admire the fact that you don't just look, act or speak
intelligently; you are brilliant; because of this,
I cannot have any negligence.

I noted how you smile; trust me, it is one of a kind; if you
don't mind,
could you smile all the time?

I cannot see how you say you are boring,

I would talk to you from night till morning; for the first time
in my life, I believe I can fly, but guess what?
I am not going to try.

I think whomever you know, talk to, whoever is your friend,
I know for a certainty just like me,

they do not want whatever you share to end

if you don't know it by now, you are genuinely

EXCEPTIONAL.

The Proposal

I solved a mystery
I want to share; I think it's a true history
because it is too good to bear.

The clues weren't hard to find,

they are right there in front of everyone's eyes; one could see
even if he were blind, anyone could win the noble prize.
At first, I couldn't comprehend; if it was true,
I wondered day and night
if it would ever end,
then you told me you would never make me blue.

I am convinced that love is powerful; it makes me feel like a
king
like I will always win; that is why I am giving you this RING!

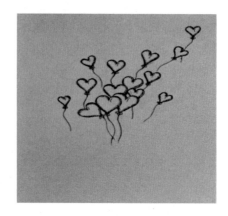

Everlasting Love

Some people think love is hard to find, hard to maintain

at times, I think they are correct,

but when I think of you,

I believe that yes, everlasting love is true.

Through the years… the hard times, the good, bad, and the sad

times,

it is not just mere luck that has kept us together

No, it was and still is our strong faith in God,

and the unceasing love for each other,

we will continue to hold firmly onto them,
and many memorable years will continue to come our way
as we continue on our journey to everlasting love.

Others

-I Will Be There for You

-Few Encouraging Words

-Yellow Roses

-Ms. Dismay

-Queen Dassa

-Late Night Musings

-Free Spirit

-Do Good

-Best Time of the Year

-Happy New Year

-Anitha's Smile

Quotes

I Will Be There for You

I will go with you through whatever you are going through,

if you want me to,

if you're down and out,

I'll be there for you.

If you're on top of the world, I'll celebrate with you; I'll try to

ease your pain when you're hurting;

I'll listen if you need to talk,

I'll pray for you and bear your burdens.

I'll cry and laugh with you; I'll be loyal to you,

wish the best for you,

and be there forever or for as long as you want me to.

Unknown

Few Encouraging Words

We all get discouraged and want to quit sometimes,

it is a part of life,

but we know, too, not to take it all so seriously, that this, too,

no matter how serious it feels, will pass

and change into another memory of someplace in life's

journey.

Remember that you are loved,

beautiful, rare, and unique, and I will always believe in you.

Unknown

Yellow Roses

Yellow roses, the color of sunshine,

I've loved you a long time,

which is why you should be mine.

The sunshine stays with us forever,

That is how long we should stay together; I will never let go,

not now, not ever.

Miss Dismay

It was a hot summer day
when I met Miss Dismay; her face showed signs of utter
frustration,
her appearance in complete disarray; my self-proclaimed
charm will be tested today.

At first, I thought she couldn't speak,

as all she did was stared at me; little did I know that she was a
beast waiting to be unleashed.

Her utterances were very much untoward,
her words piercing like a two-edged sword; remaining calm
was a struggle
as Miss Dismay went on the double.

She no longer attacked our vision

but decided,
with absolute precision, to strike at my outward appearance.

In times of war, one moment can change it all; with a smile, I politely asked,

do you have one of our cards?

Her response would make you laugh.

It is amazing how things are,

how remaining calm can solve it all; my manager called as I

packed my things. Isn't it just cliché

that Miss Dismay saved me?

Queen Dassa

Yaas goodie.

All a who want de gud up, gud up body

, The original one and only Queen Dassa deh yaa fi help yuh,

See de ockra yaa fi put wid de banga mary dem fi build up yuh

structure

Mi hav' de yellow yam fi mek yuh fast like de one Bolt

People unnu look ya, look pon dem carrot yaa

Dem fat nuh true?

Come get dem suh yuh yiy sight gud suh yuh can watch out

people bizness

Late Night Musings

The emptiness is all that is left

Sadness is my friend

Destruction, my thoughts, my words

My pen, my only friend

Nothing is all that is left of me.

Free Spirit

Hello Free Spirit, I am Timid Thoughts,

Could you take me on one of your adventures?

I'll try my utmost to be brave. Would you hold my hand and guide my way?

Hello Free Spirit, could you teach me your ways?

How to be friends with the wind, how to touch the invisible, how to speak to the waves

Hello Free Spirit, could you teach me how to smile?

How to keep running even when tired, quench my thirst from the river of life, and fill my belly with words.

Hello Free Spirit, how do I be brave? Can I be brave?

Free Spirit?

You have gone on your way.

Do Good

We are taught to be good, to do good.

The harsh reality, though, is that good may not follow us.

We can help the homeless at 10:00, and by 10:01, we could be lost or lifeless.

However, despite this harsh reality-we, we continue to do good.

The Best Time of the Year

Songs, laughter, good cheer

No need to guess the time of the year

Gifts, family, food

We all love so dear

Reflection, reminiscence

You may shed a tear

Prayer, hope

For the season to follow

There is no time for sorrow.

As we celebrate,

The best time of the year.

Happy New Year

Ladies and gents

Another year around the star

Here's your pen

Continue to write your history

Happy New Year.

Anitha's Smile

Rare, precious

A treasure worth protecting,

Anitha's Smile.

Smile so bright even the moon gets jealous

So much warmth, it is worth every mile

Feeling down? Anitha's Smile will cheer you up

I dare you to put it to the test

It doesn't matter how rough.

Anitha's Smile brings out the best.

Strength, persistence, simply powerful

It demands consistency

Simply wonderful, smile dear child

Everything is going to be all right
Be happy, be bold, be wild
With love, Anitha's Smile.

Quotes

Happiness is achieved through love, family, friendship, and memories.

Wake up! Life is Reality.

If you let your problems weigh you down, it will, and you will never get up.

The mind is mighty, it can ruin you, but it can also move mountains.

-End-

Made in the USA
Columbia, SC
13 November 2022

71150648R00020